A 30-Day Journey

UNWRAPPING THE CHRISTMAS STORY

FINDING NEW MEANING IN A FAMILIAR MESSAGE

by Debbie Kirkland

Unwrapping the Christmas Story, Finding New Meaning in a Familiar Message

Copyright © 2025 by Debbie Kirkland

All rights reserved. No parts of this book may be reproduced or used in any manner without the written permission of the copyright owner, except for the use of quotations in a book review.

Scriptures marked AMP are taken from the AMPLIFIED® BIBLE (AMP), Copyright© 1954, 1958, 1962, 1964, 1965, 1987 by the Lockman Foundation Used by Permission.

Scriptures marked ESV are taken from the ESV® Bible (The Holy Bible, English Standard Version®), copyright© 2001 by Crossway Bibles, a publishing ministry of Good News Publishers. Used by permission. All rights reserved.

Scriptures marked NIV are from THE HOLY BIBLE, NEW INTERNATIONAL VERSION®. Copyright© 1973, 1978, 1984, 2011 by Biblica, Inc.™. Used by permission of Zondervan

Scriptures marked NKJV are from the NEW KING JAMES VERSION®. Copyright© 1982 by Thomas Nelson, Inc. Used by permission. All rights reserved.

Scripture marked NLT are taken from the Holy Bible, New Living Translation, copyright ©1996, 2004, 2015 by Tyndale House Foundation. Used by permission of Tyndale House Publishers, Carol Stream, Illinois 60188. All rights reserved.

NEW AMERICAN STANDARD BIBLE - NASB 2020
Copyright (C) 1960, 1962, 1963, 1968, 1971, 1972, 1973, 1975, 1977, 1995, 2020 by THE LOCKMAN FOUNDATION A Corporation Not for Profit LA HABRA, CA All Rights Reserved

Scripture quotations marked TPT are from The Passion Translation®. Copyright © 2017, 2018, 2020 by Passion & Fire Ministries, Inc. Used by permission. All rights reserved. ThePassionTranslation.com.

ISBN 979-8-9894248-2-5

Table of Contents

Day 1	1
Day 2	3
Day 3	5
Day 4	7
Day 5	9
Day 6	11
Day 7	13
Day 8	15
Day 9	17
Day 10	19
Day 11	21
Day 12	23
Day 13	25
Day 14	27
Day 15	29
Day 16	31
Day 17	33
Day 18	35
Day 19	37
Day 20	39
Day 21	41
Day 22	43
Day 23	45

Day 24 47
The Journey 49
Day 25 53
Day 26 55
Day 27 57
Day 28 59
Day 29 61
Day 30 63
The Story Continues 65
References 66
About the Author 67

Day 1

This Christmas season, I thought I would take a journey through the Christmas story and make a note of new insights God gives me. I would like to invite you to join me over the coming days as I examine a story that is so well-known that it's easy to overlook its important truths. I hope you'll join the journey. Let's dig in.

"In the beginning [before all-time] was the Word (Christ), and the Word was with God, and the Word was God Himself." (John 1:1 AMP)

You may be saying, "Wait a minute, where's the angel talking to Mary or the manger with the wise men and shepherds?" Well, that's not where this story begins. It starts in the beginning, before time, before creation, before the world was made, and there was nothing. Jesus was there, not the man Jesus, but the second person in the Godhead Trinity. Wow! That's a hard one to wrap my head around, but I need to know this spiritual truth to fully understand the incredible story unfolding as He enters our world as a man.

Before Mary, before the manger, before the wise men and shepherds, there was the Word, and He was with God in eternity, and as God, equal to the Father. He wasn't a created being. He wasn't a lesser god.

"He existed in the beginning with God. God created everything through him, and nothing was created except through him. The Word gave life to everything that was created, and his life brought light to everyone." (John 1:2-4 NLT)

Today's incredible truth is that before Jesus became God incarnate – the most high God embodied in flesh, in human form – He was. He didn't just show up on the scene the day He was born, or even the day He was conceived. He was there before there was a beginning.

I look forward to seeing where the Holy Spirit leads us tomorrow.

Day 2

On Day 1, we explored the fact that Jesus existed before time and before He was born into the world. While we see preincarnate appearances of Jesus throughout the Old Testament, we are exploring the touch points of Him as Jesus the man. The next step we should take is to examine one of the prophecies about His coming.

"The people who walk in darkness will see a great light. For those who live in a land of deep darkness, a light will shine." (Isaiah 9:2 NLT)

Didn't we just read in Day 1, John 1:4 NLT, that His light brought light to everyone? Jesus Himself says in Revelation 22:16 NLT, "I, Jesus, have sent my angel to give you this message for the churches. I am both the source of David and the heir to his throne. I am the bright morning star." Jesus is the light that will shine on all men.

Why is Jesus being the light of the world so important? In Chapter 8 of Isaiah, the prophet warns the people of Israel and Judah of the impending Assyrian invasion that would ultimately lead to their captivity in Babylon. In Isaiah 8:20-22, he tells them that they are completely in the dark if they don't follow God's instructions and teachings but contradict them. They are told they will be weary and hungry, and because they are hungry, they will rage and curse their king and their God. They will look up to heaven and down at the earth, but wherever they look, there will be trouble, anguish, and dark despair. They will be thrown out into the darkness. Whoa! Is there no hope?

"Nevertheless, that time of darkness and despair will not go on forever…" (Isaiah 9:1a NLT)

Deep breath. Sigh of relief. So, when will this end? Well, the prophecy that comes next won't come to pass for about seven hundred years. But it will come. Those plunged into deep darkness will see a great light when Jesus comes: God incarnate, God with us. Only He can bring light back into the world. Only He can save the people from the deep darkness they've been plunged into.

It wasn't just the people in Isaiah's time. They remained in darkness for seven hundred years, looking for a Messiah who would come and save them. On this side of Jesus' coming, there are still those walking in deep darkness without His light, even though His light is right there to shine on them.

Today's truth is that we are all plunged into deep darkness without the light of Jesus. If He had not come, there would be no hope of walking out of it.

Thank you, Jesus, that You did not leave us helplessly wandering in darkness.

Day 3

"For a child is born to us, a Son is given to us. The government will rest on his shoulders. And he will be called Wonderful Counselor, Mighty God, Everlasting Father, Prince of Peace. His government and its peace will never end. He will rule with fairness and justice from the throne of his ancestor David for all eternity. The passionate commitment of the Lord of Heaven's Armies will make this happen! (Isaiah 9:6-7 NLT)

"For a child is born to us…" Jesus had to be born in order to identify fully as a human. He became a man. Only a man could be qualified to be the Messiah, our Savior and High Priest. He was fully man.

"…a Son is given to us." Jesus is also the eternal Son of God. According to David Guzik's commentary on this verse, Jesus had to be perfect and infinite to offer an infinite atonement for our sins. The humanity of Jesus had a starting point. He is fully God and fully man. The Son was given, and at that moment, human nature was added to His divine nature.

This is a very familiar prophecy about Jesus. The hymn is running through my head. I can hear the Christmas choir singing it right now. Of course, looking back from this side of the timeline, we understand it. We know it's Jesus he's talking about. We know He'll come as a baby in a manger, start His ministry at 30, do many amazing miracles, be shunned by the Jewish leaders, and eventually be condemned to death. He will be crucified and will rise again from the dead. Through all that, He will try to get His disciples to see and understand that He is ushering in a Kingdom that is not of this world.

I can see how the disciples and all who had been looking forward to their Messiah coming were thinking that He would come and set up His government here on earth, wipe out those pesky Romans, and everyone else who was oppressing them. But Jesus was coming for so much more. He was coming not only to set the Jewish people free but to set all men free, Jew and Gentile. They thought their oppressor was a foreign government. Jesus knew that governments come and go. Nations and kingdoms rise and fall. It was sin, the original sin, that had unleashed sin and death into the world to bring darkness and oppression that had to be vanquished. Then and only then could those who believe in Jesus be set free and enter a Kingdom that will never end—a Kingdom and a government that rests on His shoulders.

The last line in verse seven above says, "The passionate commitment of the Lord of Heaven's Armies will make this happen!" And He did. Jesus fulfilled this prophecy written about Himself seven hundred years before He walked the earth, as well as over three hundred other prophecies about the Messiah. When we see this fulfillment, we can rest assured that everything else written in His Word will come to pass. It may not look like we imagine, but it will be even better.

Today's truth is that God, the Lord of Heaven's Armies, can and will fulfill every promise He's made. His Kingdom will never end. He will rule from the throne of David for eternity.

Day 4

On Day 3, we discussed the prophecy given about Jesus in Isaiah, given about 700 years before He stepped onto the world scene. Today, we will begin our examination of Jesus' entry as we study Matthew Chapter One.

"All those listed above include fourteen generations from Abraham to David, fourteen from David to the Babylonian exile, and fourteen from the Babylonian exile to the Messiah." (Matthew 1:17 NLT)

Maybe you're different, but I always skipped over the long genealogy in verses one through sixteen. I mean, sixteen verses of hard-to-pronounce names are not in my top reading desires, but they serve a vital role in proving that Jesus was qualified to be the Messiah. He had to be in the line of David, and He was.

Backstory matters. We all want to know how the story began. Although Matthew doesn't give me all the details I'd like, he does start with some important ones.

"This is how Jesus the Messiah was born. His mother, Mary, was engaged to be married to Joseph. But before the marriage took place, while she was still a virgin, she became pregnant through the power of the Holy Spirit. Joseph, to whom she was engaged, was a righteous man and did not want to disgrace her publicly, so he decided to break the engagement quietly." (Matthew 1:18-19 NLT)

Joseph and Mary were engaged to be married, but being engaged in that day was not as casual as our engagements are now. To be engaged or betrothed as a Jew at that time meant that a contract had been signed, agreements had been made, and they were basically married, except she remained with her parents, usually for a year, as her betrothed went to his father's house and built a room to bring his bride home. Once that was finished, and his father said he was ready, he would get his bride, and there would be a final ceremony and consummation of the vows. Mary was in the waiting time; a virgin and contractually bound to Joseph.

Now she's pregnant—a genuine scandal. Adultery was punishable by death. Joseph could have had her stoned, but God had chosen a righteous man for Mary, and he didn't want to disgrace her publicly. He decided to break the engagement quietly. Joseph didn't know he would play a critical role in protecting Mary and the Messiah she carried. God had other plans, as we'll see in tomorrow's reading.

Today's truth is that God didn't just choose Mary to be the mother of Jesus; He also chose Joseph. Mary couldn't do this alone.

Day 5

Day 4 was a page-turner. Mary, a virgin contractually bound to marry Joseph, comes up pregnant. He is not the father. Joseph could have had her stoned for adultery, but he is kind and righteous and is contemplating his plan to break off the engagement quietly. I wish I knew more about their love story. Did he love Mary, or was he just the kind of guy who always wanted to do the right thing? He didn't have to love her. With arranged marriages, we don't know if he really knew her at all. All we know is that he was a righteous man with a really big problem to solve.

"As he considered this, an angel of the Lord appeared to him in a dream. 'Joseph, son of David,' the angel said, 'do not be afraid to take Mary as your wife. For the child within her was conceived by the Holy Spirit." (Matthew 1:20 NLT)

Joseph planned to quietly break off this engagement because what Mary probably told him about the angel and how she was pregnant by the Holy Spirit was surely unbelievable. Did she tell him what the angel told her about the child? If she did, he had to be thinking that this girl had some imagination. Maybe that's why he planned to do this quietly, because he thought she was a little crazy. Wouldn't you?

Then he has a dream.

Joseph was trying to fix what he thought was broken, but God wouldn't leave him there in the dark. He sent Joseph an angel of his own to let him in on the plan. The angel lets him know that Mary isn't crazy, so he doesn't have to be afraid to go ahead and marry her. He also told him she was telling the truth about conceiving by the Holy Spirit.

Also, did you notice that the angel addresses him as Joseph, son of David? This is important. Even though Joseph wasn't the true biological father of this child, it was still legally critical for him to be a descendant of David. He doesn't know it yet, but this is also his ticket back to Bethlehem at just the right time for Jesus to be born there; another prophecy that He will fulfill, which we'll examine later.

Today's truth is that our plans are not always God's plans. In times of trouble or crisis, God can provide wisdom and direction that lead us into His purposes and plans for our lives. We must take time to seek Him today for those answers.

Day 6

Crisis averted. Mary is pregnant, but now Joseph knows everything she told him is true. It took an angel coming to him in a dream to change his mind, but Joseph needed to be fully on board with this plan. He had to know it was real, and he needed to be told what he should do. Mary had to carry and give birth to the Messiah, but Joseph also had his part to play in this.

"And she will have a son, and you are to name him Jesus, for he will save His people from their sins. All of this occurred to fulfill the Lord's message through His prophet: "Look! The virgin will conceive a child! She will give birth to a Son, and they will call him Immanuel, which means 'God is with us.'" (Matthew 1:21-22 NLT)

". . . you are to name him Jesus." Jesus was a common name at the time, but it meant "The salvation of Yahweh." Peter says in Acts 4:12 NIV, "... there is no other name under heaven by which we must be saved."

He was to be named Jesus, the salvation of Yahweh, because He would save His people from their sins. He was coming as a savior. That was His purpose. It had been God's plan from the beginning.

As we discussed on Day 3, the people were looking for a Messiah who would come and liberate them from their oppressors. However, here, the angel makes it clear what Jesus was coming for: He was coming to save them from their sins. Another man might be able to defeat their foes, but only Jesus could save mankind from the grip of sin and death.

Paul tells us that through one man, Adam, sin and death entered the world. (Romans 5:12 NIV) Sin and its consequences spread to everyone. It is now a part of our DNA. We are helpless enemies of God because of that sin. That is why Jesus had to come into the world as a human. He had to die to take our place so that through His death and resurrection, we would receive God's wonderful grace and His gift of forgiveness through Jesus Christ. He was sinless, and He defeated death.

The mother of the Messiah had to be a virgin who conceived by the Holy Spirit because the corrupt seed of Adam could not be passed on to Him. He was truly Immanuel, God with us! The angel was letting Joseph know that the child Mary carried was the very child foretold by the prophet Isaiah. His mind had to be blown.

Today's truth is that the Christmas story isn't a sweet story about a tiny baby born in a manger. It's an incredible story of a promise fulfilled, as grace and forgiveness poured out, when God became one of us to save us from sin and death.

Day 7

The angel told Joseph that the child within Mary was conceived by the Holy Spirit, that she would have a son, and that he was to name Him Jesus because He would save His people from their sins. This was already big news, but what the angel said next was even more amazing.

So, all this was done that it might be fulfilled which was spoken by the Lord through the prophet, saying: "Behold, the virgin will be with child, and bear a Son, and they shall call His name Immanuel," which is translated, "God with us." (Matthew 1:22-23 NKJV)

Not only were Joseph and Mary supposed to wrap their head around the fact that she was carrying a child conceived by the Holy Spirit while she was still a virgin, but it was happening just as Isaiah prophesied it over 700 years before. They would have known this prophecy, and now they are a part of its fulfillment.

"When Joseph woke up, he did as the angel of the Lord commanded and took Mary as his wife. But he did not have sexual relations with her until her son was born. And Joseph named him Jesus." (Matthew 1:24-25 NLT)

When Joseph woke up, he could have thought, *Wow, that was a crazy dream,* but he didn't. He did just what the angel of the Lord commanded him to do. The angel didn't just ask him to do these things; he commanded him to do them. That could have played a part in Joseph getting up and actively obeying.

Remember, we read that Joseph was a righteous man. Well, that word in Greek is *dikaios*, which means "righteous, observing divine laws, virtuous, and keeping the commands of God. Used of him whose way of thinking, feeling, and acting is wholly conformed to the will of God." He wasn't just a good guy; he was a guy who was going to do what God told him to do. It's a good thing, too, because Joseph would have a few more encounters with that angel, and it wouldn't be an easy road ahead.

When the angel said to take Mary as his wife, he was to bring her home to live with him. He was going to be responsible for her and the child now. Did Mary tell her parents? Did they believe her? Did Joseph tell them about his dream with the angel? Or were Mary and Joseph talked about by their village as a couple who couldn't wait for the ceremony? Since Joseph took Mary as his wife, they had to think that he was the father of the child she carried.

Their reputations were probably ruined. They lived in a small village. Gossip about them was surely rampant. But this young couple was so committed to this incredible journey God had put them on that, in the face of all this, they remained true to their mission and kept Mary a virgin until the birth of Jesus.

Today's truth is that you can be smack dab in the big middle of the perfect will of God, and life can be incredibly hard around you. I wonder if Mary was the first one to tell James, Jesus' brother, to "count it all joy when you fall into various trials?" (James 1:2a NKJV)

Day 8

Let's back up just a little bit. After visiting John, Chapter 1, and learning that Jesus existed as the second person in the Godhead before time began, and then heading over to Isaiah to examine the prophecies foretelling the birth of Jesus, we jumped into Matthew. Matthew began the story with Jesus' genealogy and went straight to Joseph and Mary. But there was an angel visitation a few months before Joseph and Mary had theirs. So, we will head over to Luke and do some digging there. We will examine the story of Zechariah and Elizabeth over the next few days. There are too many details to dig through to give it just one day. Today, however, we will take a peek at how Luke begins his book.

"Since many have undertaken to compile an account of the things accomplished among us, just as they were handed down to us by those who from the beginning were eyewitnesses and servants of the word, it seemed fitting to me as well, having investigated everything carefully from the beginning, to write it out for you in an orderly sequence, most excellent Theophilus; so that you may know the exact truth about the things you have been taught." (Luke 1:1-4 NASB2020)

He's not about to tell us some fairy tale stories. Someone didn't make them up. No, these are real people with real lives who experienced incredible things. Luke tells us that he carefully searched out and investigated all the events he shares in this book from the beginning.

Luke was a doctor. He had experience examining evidence, but in case anyone thought he was just a regular guy doing amateur sleuthing, he wrote these first four verses in technically beautiful Greek. It was written in classical Greek, as classical Greek historians would open up their histories. By writing this way, Luke let everyone know he knew his stuff. He's a scholar. Then, in verse five, he starts talking in common street Greek. He establishes his credentials as a scholar with legitimate research and investigation chops and then writes a story for everyone.

Why does that matter? Well, as I said above, these weren't made-up stories. Luke examined the evidence and wrote the exact truth that could be backed up by those who lived it. It enables us to confidently interpret these accounts in light of what we've been taught. As he tells Theophilus, he's writing this book so that we may know the certainty of our faith in Jesus Christ.

Today's truth is that the Christmas story details we are examining over these thirty days are real events on which we can base our lives. We can be certain that the teachings we have received from these scriptures are true.

Day 9

As I said on Day 8, before the angel visitation to Mary and Joseph, there was a visitation a few months earlier. This visitation also announced the birth of a child, and he would play a significant role in preparing the way for Jesus. There were prophecies written about this child, too.

"Behold, I am sending My messenger, and he will clear a way before Me. And the Lord, whom you are seeking, will suddenly come to His temple; and the messenger of the covenant, in whom you delight, behold, He is coming," says the Lord of armies. (Malachi 3:1 NASB2020)

Today, we will examine Zechariah and Elizabeth, the parents of this special child. In verses 5-7, Luke tells us that during the time of Herod, king of Judea, a priest named Zechariah from the priestly division of Abijah was serving. Zechariah's wife was also in the priestly line of Aaron. They were righteous in God's eyes and observed all His commands and decrees without fault. They were the perfect couple, but there was one problem: they couldn't have a child and were both too old to have one now.

Since I've read ahead and know the end of the story, I know that Luke bringing up Herod here isn't just to let us know when all this took place. This is an introduction to the villain who will play a part in this unfolding story. Additionally, it is worth noting that Zechariah is a priest from the division of Abijah. And God doesn't leave out the women in the story either; He tells us that Elizabeth is from a very important priestly line.

But then you read that they are childless and have been for a long time. Since I already let the cat out of the bag and told you they would have a son who would prepare the way for Jesus, you already know about the first miracle in this Christmas story. So how did it begin?

"Once, when Zechariah's division was on duty and he was serving as priest before God, he was chosen by lot, according to the custom of the priesthood, to go into the temple of the Lord and burn incense. And when the time for the burning of incense came, all the assembled worshipers were praying outside." (Luke 1:8-10 NIV)

You might think that Zechariah going into the Temple and burning incense was something he did regularly, but the truth is, a priest might only get to serve in this capacity once in a lifetime. The priests who served in the Temple had to be from a certain lineage. Since there were so many of them by this time, they used a lot system to determine which priest would serve when and how. There were more jobs in the morning and evening sacrifices than burning incense, which was very special. The priest would enter with the other priests into the Holy Place. Once the other priests had finished their tasks and left, the priest offering the incense would place it on the altar and offer prayers for the nation, while the people would be outside, praying. This is what happened on this day. Tomorrow, we'll unpack what happened next.

Today's truth is that you may think all the details in your life are random, just like the lot system, but God has a plan for your life, and the details matter.

Day 10

On Day 9, we left with Zechariah being chosen by lot to burn incense in the Temple. This was a once-in-a-lifetime honor. Zechariah had probably dreamed of this day. He was an old man, so he may have thought this honor had passed him by. There were thousands of priests, and so few were chosen each year that he could have lived a lifetime without having this opportunity. Now, here he is in the Holy Place, burning incense and offering prayers for the nation of Israel.

"Then an angel of the Lord appeared to him, standing at the right side of the altar of incense. When Zechariah saw him, he was startled and was gripped with fear. But the angel said to him: 'Do not be afraid, Zechariah; your prayer has been heard.'" (Luke 1:11-13a NIV)

While angels are mentioned more in the New Testament than love and sin, this doesn't mean everyone saw them. Zechariah probably felt like his heart skipped a beat. I think it's a pretty good description that, at first, he was startled; he thought he was alone there, and then, when he realizes it's a huge angel standing there, he's terrified. I think we all would be.

The angel tells him not to be afraid, but then says something interesting: Your prayer has been heard. At first reading, I thought the angel might be referring to his prayer for a child, since that's what he was there to tell him, but his job at that moment was to offer prayers for his nation. He was a righteous man, a priest, and this was a lifetime opportunity; he wouldn't be there asking for his personal needs. Plus, as an old man, he wouldn't have been praying for a child anymore, and certainly not at this momentous occasion, but God is so good. He not only answered his prayer for his nation – John was going to usher in and prepare the way for the Messiah, but He was also going to answer many years of prayers for Zechariah personally.

"Your wife Elizabeth will bear you a son; you are to call him John. He will be a joy and delight to you, and many will rejoice because of his birth, for he will be great in the sight of the Lord." (Luke 1:13b-15a NIV)

The angel begins by stating that this answer to his prayer will be for his own personal joy and delight, but then he expands it to include others. Many will rejoice because of this child's birth. And not only will he be a joy and a delight to many, but he will also be great in the sight of the Lord. This promise would be amazing on its own, but tomorrow, we will see that there's much more.

Today's truth is that we never know if our waiting is for a much bigger purpose than we ever imagined. Our prayers are never wasted, whether they are for ourselves or others. God cares about them all.

Day 11

On Day 10, we saw Zechariah in the Holy Place burning incense and praying for his nation. He was probably praying with his eyes closed, and then he opened them, and boom, an angel stood there at the right side of the incense altar. He's startled at first because he's supposed to be in there alone, but upon closer examination, this guy is really powerful and scary-looking. He's more than startled; he's terrified now. Gabriel tells him not to be afraid, then goes into his message. You, Zechariah, will have a son; you are to name him John, and he will bring joy and delight to not just you but lots of people. He will be great in the sight of the Lord, and then he tells him the big deal about John. He's not going to be some ordinary kid.

"He is never to take wine or other fermented drink, and he will be filled with the Holy Spirit even before he is born. He will bring back many of the people of Israel to the Lord their God. And he will go on before the Lord, in the spirit and power of Elijah, to turn the hearts of the parents to their children and the disobedient to the wisdom of the righteous—to make ready a people prepared for the Lord." (Luke 1:15b-17 NIV)

For John not to take wine or other fermented drink means that he is called to be a Nazarite, as described in Numbers 6:2. Many people would make a Nazarite vow for a period of time, but John is to be specially consecrated to God for his whole life. Not only that, but he will be filled with the Holy Spirit in the womb. He will be all of this because he has a huge job to do. John's mission would be to prepare the hearts of the people of Israel for their Messiah by bringing them back to the Lord their God.

Before I go into the next thing said about John, I want to say it blows my mind how God told His prophet about John's life 700 years before he was born, then he told Zechariah before he was even conceived all about the life he would live and the things he would do, and they happened just as God said!

Okay, back to the story. Let's look back to the prophet Malachi and the last words spoken by God at the end of the Old Testament, before a 400-year period of silence.

"Look, I am sending you the prophet Elijah before the great and dreadful day of the LORD arrives. His preaching will turn the hearts of fathers to their children, and the hearts of children to their fathers. Otherwise, I will come and strike the land with a curse." (Malachi 4:5-6 NLT)

Sound familiar? God speaks, then remains silent for 400 years. Now, he's saying it again about this baby that is about to be conceived and brought into the world. Jesus confirms in Matthew 11:14 and 17:12 that John came in the power of Elijah just as it was foretold. Definitely not an ordinary child sent to bring joy to Zechariah and Elizabeth in their old age. No, he was coming to prepare the way of the Lord, but he will bring joy while he's doing it.

Today's truth is that God knows the details of time from beginning to end. He knows everything about our lives before we ever live one minute, and He's right there, active in the midst of it. We can trust Him with the outcome.

Day 12

Zechariah and Elizabeth had no children. It's obvious from later in this story that this was not a choice they made; it was a reproach to them. At that time, being barren was looked at as a judgment of God. People thought you probably had some secret sin in your life. Now, the angel tells Zechariah that Elizabeth will bear him a son, and this child will be extraordinary. So, is Zechariah dancing in the streets from this news? Let's see.

"Zechariah asked the angel, 'How can I be sure of this? I am an old man, and my wife is well along in years.'" (Luke 1:18 NIV)

Basically, he's telling the angel that he thinks this is impossible because… *Have you seen us? We are too old to have kids. Are you messing with me? We've never been able to have kids.* On the one hand, you can't blame him; God hadn't been speaking for the last 400 years, so angels weren't regularly giving people big messages like this. Plus, after a lifetime of praying for his biggest heart's desire, he had given up believing that God would answer that prayer a long time ago. On the other hand, this heavenly being is standing right in front of him, bringing this message. The angel told him quickly that he wasn't too happy with Zechariah's doubts about his message.

"The angel said to him, 'I am Gabriel. I stand in the presence of God, and I have been sent to speak to you and to tell you this good news. And now you will be silent and not able to speak until the day this happens because you did not believe my words, which will come true at their appointed time.'" (Luke 1:19-20 NIV)

Zechariah could only see his circumstances and the impossibility of them. Gabriel was bringing very good news, and he didn't believe him. He told him who he was and his incredible credentials for bringing this message. He stands in the presence of God, and if God says it, it will come to pass. Then, he silences Zechariah before he can speak any other words of unbelief. This was God's plan, and as the angel said, it would come true at the appointed time, regardless of whether Zechariah had the faith to make it happen or not. Thankfully, it was about fulfilling God's plan and promise, not Zechariah's faith.

Today's truth is this, "…if we are faithless, he remains faithful—for He cannot deny Himself." (2 Timothy 2:13 ESV)

Day 13

In Luke 1:21-22, we see the people waiting and wondering why Zechariah is taking so long. When a priest entered the Holy Place and burned incense on the altar, the people waiting outside could see the smoke rise through the roof of the Temple. They would then know that the priest was offering prayers, and the assembly would fall to their faces and pray until the priest came out to pray a blessing over them, and it would be over. When Zechariah finally came out, the people realized he had seen a vision because he kept making signs and was unable to speak.

"When Zechariah's week of service in the Temple was over, he returned home. Soon afterward, his wife, Elizabeth, became pregnant and went into seclusion for five months. 'How kind the Lord is!' she exclaimed. 'He has taken away my disgrace of having no children.'" (Luke 1:23-25 NLT)

Zechariah had to continue working in the Temple for the entire week. While the priests were on duty, they were unable to go home. He had to be anxious to get home to Elizabeth and try to explain somehow all that had happened to him in the Holy Place. Thankfully, they didn't have to wait long before they saw evidence that what the angel said was coming true. Was he shocked, or had he gone home and had relations with his wife as an act of belief and obedience to the word given? I'd like to believe he chose to believe Gabriel and was partnering with the Lord to enable the promise to happen. He did his part and waited on the Lord to do His.

Nothing in the text or biblical culture tells us why Elizabeth secluded herself for five months upon learning she was pregnant. Does she feel protective of this child and not ready to bring the world into this marvelous gift just yet? Is she waiting until there is no denying that she is pregnant to let people know? Her whole married life, she's been barren, and with that came shame and disgrace. She could have hesitated to set herself up for public ridicule, even if it would be for a short time. She may not have wanted voices of doubt and unbelief spoken over her or the child. She chose to remain silent about this miracle along with her husband.

Whatever reason Elizabeth had for going into seclusion, we will see in the coming verses that she didn't have to finish the last three months of her pregnancy alone.

Today's truth is that we may have moments of unbelief, but when we choose to believe and partner with God, being obedient to our part of the equation, amazing things happen.

Day 14

Today, we will begin to examine the story of Mary and Joseph. We've already looked at the story from the report in Matthew, but let's look at what Luke has to say about Mary and her visit from the angel Gabriel.

"Now in the sixth month [of Elizabeth's pregnancy], the angel Gabriel was sent from God to a city in Galilee called Nazareth, to a virgin betrothed to a man whose name was Joseph, a descendant of the house of David; and the virgin's name was Mary. And coming to her, he said, 'Greetings, favored one! The Lord is with you.' But she was very perplexed at what he said and kept carefully considering what kind of greeting this was. The angel said to her, "Do not be afraid, Mary, for you have found favor with God." (Luke 1:26-31 AMP)

Gabriel was sent from God to Nazareth. In this translation, it is referred to as a city, but commentators note that Nazareth was an obscure village in the Region of Galilee. This is the first time it's mentioned in the Old and New Testaments. It's far from everything and has no acclaim to it. It seems strange that God would use such a small, unknown place to identify Christ. Multiple scriptures refer to Jesus as 'Jesus of Nazareth.' In John 1:46 NKJV, Nathanael asks, "Can anything good come out of Nazareth?" John's birth announcement came to a priest in the Temple in Jerusalem, and yet our Savior's birth announcement came to an obscure village in the middle of nowhere to a young girl. In God's economy, no person or place is too unknown or obscure for Him.

This young girl, a virgin betrothed to a man named Joseph, is the one to whom the angel was sent. Her name is Mary, meaning 'exalted one.' She will be exalted at some point in man's eyes, but I'm sure Mary has never seen herself in that way. She's a poor girl in a small village just living her life, preparing for her marriage to Joseph. An angel appears and declares a remarkable greeting, calling her "favored one" and saying, "The Lord is with you." What strikes me in this account is that Mary doesn't seem terrified like Zechariah when she sees the angel. She's perplexed by what he says and carefully considers what this kind of greeting means. When the angel says, "Do not be afraid, Mary," is he saying this because he thinks she is afraid of him, or does he see her concern over the greeting and what it may mean for her? This shows me that Mary was not some frivolous, silly young girl. No, she is a thinker, and this is the first of many times she will ponder the events around her in her heart.

Mary has found favor with God. He has seen her and chosen her to be the mother of His Son. She will need to hang on to these words in the coming days.

Today's truth is that we are never too hidden for God to see and move in our lives.

Day 15

In yesterday's post, I contemplated whether Gabriel told Mary not to be afraid because he thought she was afraid of him or if he knew she was concerned about his greeting and what it meant to her. Another thought came to me that maybe he was telling her not to fear what she was about to hear. This will be news that will change the course of history, and her life will never be the same.

"Listen carefully: you will conceive in your womb and give birth to a son, and you shall name Him Jesus. He will be great and eminent and will be called the Son of the Most High; and the Lord will give Him the throne of His father David, and He will reign over the house of Jacob (Israel) forever, and of His kingdom, there shall be no end." (Luke 1:31-33 AMP)

Do you think Gabriel is telling her to stop worrying about his greeting and focus on what he's about to say? "Listen carefully." Other versions say, "And behold," but any way you say it, I still think he was telling her to focus before he dropped the most incredible news on her: that she would conceive and give birth to God's Son. This is the most important news anyone will ever hear, and she must pay attention.

She is to name this child Jesus. As I mentioned in an earlier post, Jesus was a common name at the time, but it means 'The Salvation of Yahweh.' The description of Him will point to all that He will be. His name won't just mean the Salvation of Yahweh; He will **BE** the Salvation of Yahweh.

He will be given David's throne just as the prophecies of the Messiah have said, and He will reign over the house of Jacob forever. His kingdom will have no end. By this point, Mary may realize that she is the virgin referred to in those prophecies, and the son she will give birth to will be the Messiah they've waited for and watched for all these years.

The angel's encouragement to not be afraid is very powerful about now. She's young and unmarried, and the task before her is daunting. Was Mary afraid? Was she excited? Did she understand at this moment the full ramifications of everything? Whatever her emotions, according to the angel, the Lord is with her; she is highly favored and needn't be afraid.

Today's truth is we have nothing to fear, either. As we celebrate the birth of our Savior during this season, let's remember who we are in Him and all that He has promised us. Like Mary, God is with us. Jesus said, "I am with you always, to the end of the age (Matthew 28:20 NASB2020), we are blessed with every spiritual blessing in the heavenly places (Ephesians 1:3 NKJV), and we are favored; he has blessed us with His glorious grace in the Beloved (Ephesians 1:6 NASB2020), meaning we have His divine grace which is His undeserved love and favor.

Day 16

Gabriel appeared to her and said, "Greetings, favored woman! The Lord is with you! (Luke 1:28 NLT)

Mary was favored. Why? What was it about her that caught God's attention? Why did He choose her to be the mother of His Son? Did she do something special, or did He pick her out of a group of girls her age who were descendants of David?

Reading further, we can find many clues as to why God chose Mary.

The angel of the Lord visited her and told her she would conceive a son and name him Jesus. He would be great, called the Son of the Most High, given the throne of David, and reign over Israel forever. Mary's response is important.

"Mary asked the angel, 'How will this be, since I am a virgin?'" (Luke 1:34 NLT)

At first, this may seem to be the same kind of response Zechariah had, but she wants to know how it will happen physically for her. She is a virgin. She was asking, "What will I have to do to conceive this baby?"

We know her response was different because Gabriel's response was different.

"The angel replied, 'The Holy Spirit will come upon you, and the power of the Most High will overshadow you. So the baby to be born will be holy, and he will be called the Son of God.'" (Luke 1:35 NLT)

"Mary responded, 'I am the Lord's servant. May everything you have said about me come true.'" And then the angel left her. (Luke 1:38 NLT)

What all this meant for her was that she would be pregnant and unmarried, and her fiancé, Joseph, would know it wasn't his. Would anyone believe her story? She could have been stoned for adultery, but she still said yes. Why? We will explore that tomorrow.

Today's truth is that Mary said yes to the Lord's request even when the ramifications were formidable. She didn't hesitate but took the position of being the Lord's servant.

Day 17

There were two verses in the middle of the angel telling Mary about Jesus, and her response that we didn't look at. They are important and may have contributed to Mary's prompt response.

"And listen, even your relative Elizabeth has also conceived a son in her old age, and she who was called barren is now in her sixth month. For with God nothing [is or ever] shall be impossible." (Luke 1:36-37 AMP)

Mary would have known about Elizabeth's disgrace of being barren all those years. She would have known her time had passed, but now the angel is telling her about this impossible gift that hadn't just happened, but had been in place for six months. Mary is young and hasn't had a lifetime of disappointments to cloud her wonder and awe of the things she is hearing.

The angel told her what would happen to her, and he also informed her about what had already happened to her relative. The only thing left is for her to answer, and she says *Yes, let everything you've said about me come true.*

In the next few verses, we see Mary immediately heading to visit Zechariah and Elizabeth. Did she want to see for herself that Elizabeth was pregnant, or, more likely, did she need to tell someone she knew would believe her and help support her in this situation?

At the sound of Mary's voice, the child Elizabeth is carrying leaps within her, and Elizabeth is filled with the Holy Spirit. Then Mary gets what she possibly came for: the belief that all that has happened to her is real. Mary may have needed confirmation that she wasn't crazy or dreaming.

"Elizabeth gave a glad cry and exclaimed to Mary, 'God has blessed you above all women, and your child is blessed. Why am I so honored that the mother of my Lord should visit me? When I heard your greeting, the baby in my womb jumped for joy. You are blessed because you believed that the Lord would do what He said.'" (Luke 1:42-45 NLT)

One thing Elizabeth said to her jumped out at me, "You are blessed because you believed that the Lord would do what he said." (Luke 1:45 NLT)

Mary was blessed because she believed. She believed the Lord would do all that He promised, and that it would happen just as the angel said. She's already pregnant and still a virgin, and Elizabeth is now standing in front of her, already six months pregnant. Why wouldn't she believe that everything else she was told would happen as well?

Tomorrow, we will unpack Mary's beautiful response to Elizabeth.

Today's truth is that blessings come to those who believe the Lord does what He says. God keeps His promises.

Day 18

For the past few days, we've examined why God chose Mary to be the mother of His Son. We've already seen that she is humble and willing to do whatever the Lord asks of her, even in the face of formidable circumstances. Today, as we read her beautiful Magnificat, I believe it reveals an even deeper understanding of who Mary was and why God chose her.

Mary responded,
> "Oh, how my soul praises the Lord.
> How my spirit rejoices in God, my Savior!
> For he took notice of his lowly servant girl,
> and from now on, all generations will call me blessed.
> For the Mighty One is holy,
> and he has done great things for me.
> He shows mercy from generation to generation
> to all who fear him.
> His mighty arm has done tremendous things!
> He has scattered the proud and haughty ones.
> He has brought down princes from their thrones
> and exalted the humble.
> He has filled the hungry with good things
> and sent the rich away with empty hands.
> He has helped his servant Israel
> and remembered to be merciful.

> For he made this promise to our ancestors,
> to Abraham and his children forever."
> (Luke 1:46-55 NLT)

There it is, right there! Mary knew the covenant promises of God, and she already believed they would come to pass. She didn't just know them; she believed them. She already knew about all He had done. Her praises are filled with references to the Law, the Psalms, and the Prophets.

Mary wasn't just another Israelite girl of the right age and lineage. She was a girl whose heart was filled with the Word of God! So, when God called on her to be the vessel to bring His Son into the world, she was ready and willing.

Today's truth is our God is worthy of all our praise and honor! He is mighty to save and has done great things for us.

Day 19

Luke 1:56 tells us that Mary stayed with Elizabeth for about three months and then went home. It doesn't tell us if she stayed for the birth of John or left before he was born. Since she arrived when Elizabeth was six months pregnant and stayed with her for three months, you would assume she remained until the baby was born. Was this a preparation time for her own pregnancy and delivery?

"When it was time for Elizabeth's baby to be born, she gave birth to a son. And when her neighbors and relatives heard that the Lord had been very merciful to her, everyone rejoiced with her. When the baby was eight days old, they all came for the circumcision ceremony. They wanted to name him Zechariah, after his father. But Elizabeth said, 'No, His name is John!' 'What,' they exclaimed. 'There is no one in all your family by that name.' So, they used gestures to ask the baby's father what he wanted to name him. He motioned for a writing tablet, and to everyone's surprise, he wrote, 'His name is John.' Instantly, Zechariah could speak again, and he began praising God." (Luke 1:59-64 NLT)

Elizabeth had a boy, just as God had promised she would. All the neighbors and relatives rejoiced with them, just as Gabriel had told them would happen. Now came the naming of the child. Since Zechariah could not speak, the crowd assumed they knew what he would want this boy to be named: Zechariah, of course. Elizabeth is quick and adamant that his name is John. They acted as if she were crazy and then asked Zechariah what he wanted to name him. You can't blame them for not understanding why Elizabeth would name the child some name that wasn't attached to their family. In any other instance, Zechariah would have wanted the boy he had waited for all these years to have his name.

It's puzzling why they would use gestures to ask Zechariah since he was not deaf but merely mute. Since he communicated with gestures, it may have seemed natural to talk to him using gestures as well. He quickly let them know his son's name was John. This was an act of faith and obedience for Zechariah. He may have doubted the initial announcement, but it is clear here that he no longer doubted the promise God had given him. God was faithful to return his voice, and the first thing he did was praise the God who keeps His promises. He was filled with the Holy Spirit and prophesied about God's goodness, power to save, mercy, and much more.

Awe struck everyone, and they spread the news through the Judean hills, and those who heard the story wondered what this special child would turn out to be. It was evident to everyone that God had His hand on this boy.

The last verse in this chapter tells us that "John grew up and became strong in spirit. And he lived in the wilderness until he began his public ministry in Israel." (Luke 1:80 NLT)

Today's truth is that if God says it will happen, it does. When we examine the Word of God, we see prophecies spoken centuries before they are fulfilled, yet they are fulfilled. We see others spoken, and in a short time, it happens. If story after story shows us evidence that God is faithful to what He says He will do, we can be sure that every promise in His Word that hasn't been fulfilled yet is on its way.

Day 20

Expectation

My lack of expectation could have cost me the child I had longed for. Decades of dashed hopes and the disgrace of barrenness had hardened my heart and caused me to lose hope that my prayers would ever be answered. Now, as I stand here holding this miracle of God, I think back to that life-changing day.

It started as any other day with my order of priests on duty for the week. I had been chosen by lot to enter the sanctuary of the Lord and burn incense. I hadn't been in the Holy place for long before he appeared, a huge angel of the Lord standing to the right of the incense altar. I was so overwhelmed by fear that I almost couldn't stand. He told me not to fear and called me by my name, Zechariah. Then he started telling me the wildest story – Elizabeth would give me a son, and we were to call him John. He went on to describe the boy and all he would do. It sounded incredible, but didn't he realize how old Elizabeth and I were? How could this possibly be true?

I realize now that he could have struck me down dead right then and there. What a fool I was. How was I doubting this when I was looking right into the eyes of this angelic being? Instead of striking me dead, he let me know that he was Gabriel, and he stands in the very presence of God. God Himself had sent him to tell me this good news. But now that I had not believed him, I would be silent and unable to speak until the child was born. It didn't matter that I had doubts; God was still faithful to His promise, which would be fulfilled in its proper time.

The other priests were waiting for me and had begun to worry that something was wrong. When I walked out and couldn't speak, they knew something had happened. I finally got them to understand that I had seen a vision. I'm thankful my merciful God gave me the time to regain my faith.

Now I stand here holding the son He promised we would have.

John, his name is John, and I wait with great expectation to see all that the angel told me about him come to pass.

(Luke 1:5-25; 57-79 NLT)

Day 21

We've discussed Jesus being part of the Godhead from before time began, Zechariah and Elizabeth receiving the news, and then the miracle of their son, John, who came as a forerunner to the Messiah. Mary had a visit from the angel Gabrielle, Joseph had a dream, and now we are closing in on the biggest event mankind has ever known.

Luke anchors this story once again in history. This part of the story takes place during the reign of the Roman emperor, Caesar Augustus. Quirinius was the governor of Syria at the time. Everyone was called back to the city of their tribal origin to register for the census. Real people during a real time in history, affecting the lives of many and ultimately the lives of every Jesus follower.

"And Joseph also went up from Galilee, from the town of Nazareth to Judea, to 'the city of David, which is called Bethlehem, because he was of the house and lineage of David, to be registered with Mary, his betrothed, who was with child.'" (Luke 2:4-5 NLT)

Both Joseph and Mary were from the lineage of David. Both had to return and register. This is a simple thing that we think just happened at that time. Caesar Augustus decided to decree that everyone should be registered. But we know from prophecy that Jesus was to be born in Bethlehem. Joseph and Mary wouldn't have traveled through mountainous, rocky terrain for around 70 miles on foot and riding a donkey for fun if not for this census. Especially not while Mary was close to giving birth.

Just a side note, when I first read "Mary, his betrothed…" I thought, wait a minute, Joseph took her home to be his wife. But then I realized that to move from betrothed to married, the marriage had to be consummated. That was the final step in the process. Before Jesus' birth, Mary remained a virgin, so even though she was kept and cared for by Joseph, she was still his betrothed until after the birth.

"And while they were there, the time came for her to give birth. And she gave birth to her firstborn son and wrapped him in swaddling cloths and laid him in a manger because there was no place for them in the inn." (Luke 2:6-7 NLT)

Two small verses about our Savior's birth. I have so many questions. I'm sure women at that time were the same as today and talked in detail about their birth experiences with other moms. However, Luke doesn't provide us with any details. Did Joseph help her? Did he run for a midwife? We don't have any evidence that anyone else was at the actual birth of Jesus. Luke was a doctor and could have given us so many more details about this incredible birth, but apparently, the details we have here are all we need to know.

His first bed was not in a palace with furniture made of gold and soft fabrics; the 'bread of life' was laid in a feeding trough.

Today's truth is that God the Father planned and orchestrated every tiny detail of Jesus' birth, and all the tiny details of our lives are also in His hands. I can trust that even when things don't happen as I expect, He will work everything out for my ultimate good, aligning it with His plan.

Day 22

We left off with Mary and Joseph laying Jesus in a manger. What happens next is an amazing part of this story.

"And in the same region, there were shepherds out in the field, keeping watch over their flock by night. And an angel of the Lord appeared to them, and the glory of the Lord shone around them, and they were filled with fear. And the angel said to them, 'Fear not, for behold, I bring you good news of great joy that will be for all the people. For unto you is born this day in the city of David a Savior, who is Christ the Lord. And this will be a sign for you: you will find a baby wrapped in swaddling cloths and lying in a manger.'" (Luke 2:8-12 NLT)

Bethlehem was just a few miles from Jerusalem. Most of the sheep here were used in the temple sacrifices. It must be significant that the first people who are told about Jesus' birth are the same ones who care for these sheep.

We have shepherds in the field like any other night. Suddenly, an angel appears along with the glory of the Lord. What does that mean? I think it probably means the night sky lit up as brightly as daytime. It was understandably a spectacular sight that filled them with fear. This wasn't just a big guy who walked up to their fire. Once again, the angel must tell them not to fear. Do you think he gets tired of having to lead with that instead of the great message he's carrying, or is that actually part of his message?

This good news of great joy was for all people. It still is. There is not one soul left out of the wonderful gift of Jesus. All you must do is receive it. Not only does the angel say that this news is for all people, but he also doubles down on it and tells them, "…unto you is born…" This child born in the city of David is the Savior, the Messiah, the Lord – the promised one you've waited for all these centuries. He is Lord, God, deity, and born for you. Then, the angel must give them a sign— He's wrapped in swaddling cloths and lying in a manger.

What?! These words may seem normal because we've heard this story many times, but the angel has just told them the Savior Messiah, the Lord [God], was just born. He's not in a palace somewhere; he's lying in a manger in Bethlehem, and they are invited to see Him. He's described exactly how their perfect, spotless lambs are kept for the sacrifice – wrapped in swaddling cloths and put in a manger – do they understand this sign and its significance? A shepherd caring for the spotless lambs for sacrifice just might.

Today's truth is that the proclamation of Jesus' birth is unto us as much as it was to those shepherds. Because Jesus came as Immanuel, God with us, through Him, we have peace with God and access to the salvation He offers.

Day 23

We left off with the shepherds in the field, watching their flock at night. All at once, an angel appears, as well as the glory of God shining all around them. The angel brings incredible news: the Messiah was born in Bethlehem.

"Then all at once in the night sky, a vast number of glorious angels appeared, the very armies of heaven! And they all praised God, singing:

'Glory to God in the highest realms of heaven!
For there is peace and good hope given to the sons of men.'
(Luke 2:13-14 TPT)

I think one angel with the glory of God would be absolutely amazing, but the very armies of heaven, audible and visible…whoa! This life-giving, grace-filled news required a whole choir of praise and glory to herald it. The armies of heaven couldn't contain themselves because they knew what this would mean for all people everywhere, at all times.

"When the choir of angels disappeared and returned to heaven, the shepherds said to one another, 'Let's go! Let's hurry and find this Word (in Greek, it's the word Rhema) who is born in Bethlehem and see for ourselves what the Lord has revealed to us.' So they hurried off and found their way to Mary and Joseph. And there was the baby, lying in a feeding trough." (Luke 2:15-16 TPT)

They heard the message, and they went. The invitation is still given to us today. The Word is not still lying in a manger for us to run and see, but the life-giving, grace-filled news that Jesus came to us, Immanuel, God with us, is still held out. We have the same choice the shepherds had on that night long ago: sit and marvel at the wonder of it all but do nothing, or go, hurry, run to seek out this Savior sent to set us free.

"Upon seeing this miraculous sign, the shepherds recounted what had just happened. Everyone who heard the shepherds' story was astonished by what they were told." (Luke 2:17-18 TPT)

Once we find Christ, the Messiah, it's up to us to do what the shepherds did and share our story. Everyone they shared this story with was astonished. I know not all believed. There had to be those who said, "Crazy shepherds, what are they going on about? Angels, a baby in a feeding trough, who can believe that wild story?" But there had to be others who listened and believed that night, and their lives would never be the same. I'm in the camp of believers. Which camp are you in?

Today's truth is this: when you hear the message meant for all people everywhere, at all times, you have a choice to hear and walk away or believe, receive, and go tell your story.

Day 24

The shepherds saw and heard the angel's declaration. They sought out the babe in the manger, and what they saw and heard drove them into the streets to share this incredible experience.

"The shepherds returned to their flock, ecstatic over what had happened. They praised God and glorified Him for all they had heard and seen for themselves, just like the angel had said." (Luke 2:20 TPT)

To these shepherds, the Messiah was no longer a story they had heard about all their lives. They experienced the truth for themselves and saw it was real, just as they had been told. This experience with the babe Jesus and the confirmation of all they had been told caused them to praise and glorify God.

"If the cradle of Christ had such an effect upon them, as to make them rise from the stable and the manger to heaven, how much more powerful ought the death and resurrection of Christ to be in raising us to God?" (Calvin)

"But Mary treasured all these things in her heart and often pondered what they meant." (Luke 2:19 TPT)

Once again, we see Mary responding differently from others around her. All these details aren't passing her by; she is treasuring them all in her heart and thinking of them often. All that Gabriel told her about this child, everything she heard from Elizabeth and Zechariah, now the shepherds' story and worship are all being pondered by this young mother as she considers the deeper meaning of it all. Mary had a habit of documenting all she was experiencing around this special child, Jesus. Whether she wrote it down or not, she kept track of everything.

Today's truth is that we must experience Jesus for ourselves. He can't be just a story we've heard about or some academic theology we adhere to. As we draw close to Christmas Day, when people worldwide celebrate the birth of our Savior, Jesus Christ, let us open our hearts to the truth of God with us and experience His presence in our lives.

The Journey

The journey was hard. It was rocky and steep in places. Poor Joseph had to stop for me so many times. Traveling so close to the baby's time coming was not at all what we would have chosen. Joseph often reminded me that even though Caesar Augustus called for this census, it was all in God's hands. This baby was prophesied to be born in Bethlehem, so he would.

I was afraid sometimes, but I thought of how certain the angel was when he told me all that would happen, so I held on to those promises and knew it would all work out as it should.

Bethlehem was so crowded. There were people everywhere from all over the region. We slept out in the fields close to the village for the first few nights. There were encampments all around us. Joseph made friends with a man who owned a cave where he sheltered his animals. He was so kind to give Joseph some straw for me to sleep on, so the ground wouldn't be too hard. The day the pains started, I knew I couldn't give birth in the midst of all these people. Joseph went to the Inn to try to get us a room. He begged the man, but there was no room for us there. We had almost given up any hope of having privacy when his friend with the cave offered it to us. I knew God would provide; I didn't know how.

We settled into the warm space. It wasn't ideal, but it was better than the field. The pains were coming closer together, so I knew it wouldn't be long. I was so grateful I spent those months with Elizabeth, so I would know what to expect when my time came. I wished she could have been with me then.

When the time came, it almost seemed like a dream. The baby came so fast and easily, nothing like I had heard from other mothers. Before I knew it, he was in my arms. I took out the swaddling cloths I had prepared and wrapped him snugly in them. He was the sweetest thing I'd ever seen. "I'm a mother now," was all I kept saying to myself. Even though I knew this child was very different, he was still mine. The love that flooded my heart was overwhelming. My mother told me I would feel this way, but until I did, I couldn't imagine how life-changing it would be.

Joseph was so tender. He took this child in his arms, and the look of pure joy on his face made me cry. He thought I was in pain, but I told him I was so thankful for him through it all. I understood why God chose him to be Jesus' father here. Jesus, that's the name the angel told us to give him. A name that everyone in Israel will know. They didn't know it yet, but their Savior had been born.

The night was dark, and we laid Jesus in the manger filled with fresh hay. Joseph told me to rest and sleep, and he'd keep watch. I didn't know how long I had been asleep when several men outside the cave awakened me. Joseph stepped in front of me and the manger, and asked the men what they wanted.

At first, we could hardly understand what they were saying. They were talking excitedly all at once. Finally, Joseph got them to calm down and explain one at a time why they were there. The story they finally told was almost unbelievable, but I knew it was true the moment they said it.

They had seen one angel at first, and just that one angel had lit up the field like daytime. He had told them that he came with good news that would bring great joy to all people. And then he told them that the Savior, the Messiah, had been born in Bethlehem. They were to look for a baby wrapped in swaddling cloths lying in a manger.

I sat there, taking in every word they spoke; the angel, the glory that was as bright as the sun, then the angel army that burst into the sky. Warrior angels so fierce that one would make a man fall like dead on his face, but they were singing with great joy, proclaiming this good news. The very army of heaven was singing about my baby. I would think about their story throughout the years, especially during those first hard years as we ran from Herod into Egypt. This was yet another proof that my child didn't just belong to me, but to all mankind.

Day 25

Through all the scriptures we've read about Mary, she hasn't been fearful, doubtful, amazed, or astonished. What we've seen is that she's been contemplative. She's examined and mulled over all that she's seen and heard. Why? I think it's because this isn't a one-time experience for her. She is in this for the long haul. The pregnancy and birth are only the beginning of this long journey she is on. Now, the baby has been born, the shepherds have come and gone, and it's time to get on with life.

"And when eight days were completed so that it was time for His circumcision, He was also named Jesus, the name given by the angel before He was conceived in the womb." (Luke 2:21 NASB2020)

Joseph and Mary are parents, and their job is to make sure all that needs to happen happens–circumcision and naming the baby. Both were acts of obedience. One was a command from Leviticus 12:3, and by following this command, they showed their devotion to God and enabled Jesus to fulfill the law. The second event, naming Jesus the name given to them by the angel, was an act of obedience to what they were told to do, and, like it was with Zechariah, a demonstration of their belief in all they had been told.

"And when the days of their purification according to the Law of Moses were completed, they brought Him up to Jerusalem to present Him to the Lord (as it is written in the Law of the Lord: 'Every firstborn male that opens the womb shall be called holy to the Lord'), and to offer a sacrifice according to what has been stated in the Law of the Lord: 'A pair of turtledoves or two young doves.'" (Luke 2:22-24 NASB2020)

Again, all that was needed to fulfill the law was done. While they were there in the temple, a man named Simeon, a righteous and devout man, was led by the Holy Spirit into the temple as Mary and Joseph brought Jesus in. He took Jesus into his arms, blessed God, and prophesied over Him.

"Jesus' parents were amazed at what was being said about him. Then Simeon blessed them, and he said to Mary, the baby's mother, 'This child is destined to cause many in Israel to fall, and many others to rise. He has been sent as a sign from God, but many will oppose Him. As a result, the deepest thoughts of many hearts will be revealed. And a sword will pierce your very soul.'" (Luke 2:33-35 NLT)

They were amazed at what they heard. They'd already had angel visits and heard all the shepherds had seen, so why be amazed at what Simeon was telling them? I believe the difference is that they realized they were not alone. God had set in the heart of another an understanding of who their Son was and would become. This was another piece in the puzzle that would be His life.

Today's truth is that the everyday things we need to do keep us on the path that can lead to amazing things. So many times, we stress and strive, worried we'll miss something big we think should happen, but if we stay obedient to the things we know are right, God will bring the big things to us.

Day 26

Joseph and Mary probably thought they would be unknown as they entered the temple. They were a poor young couple, just coming to the temple to complete the purification required by the law of Moses. Now Simeon has come and held their son, speaking amazing things over him, and before they can go on their way, another comes in, Anna, a prophetess. She was widowed after only seven years of marriage and has lived in the temple, fasting and praying night and day from then until now, at age 84.

"She came along just as Simeon was talking with Mary and Joseph, and she began praising God. She talked about the child to everyone who had been waiting expectantly for God to rescue Jerusalem." (Luke 2:38 NLT)

So far, we've seen that from the time of Jesus' birth, those who encountered Him ended up praising God and telling everyone they knew about Him. Let's move back into Matthew and see if everyone feels the same way.

Matthew begins chapter two, letting us know that Jesus was born in Bethlehem in Judea during the reign of King Herod. He was known for being paranoid and cruel. In fits of rage and jealous paranoia, he was reported to have killed close associates and family members. Caesar Augustus was known to say that it was safer to be Herod's pig than it was to be Herod's son.

In Matthew 2:2-4, wise men from the East arrive and start asking about the newborn king of the Jews. King Herod and everyone in Jerusalem, aka the leaders, are deeply disturbed when they hear this. We know that Simeon and Anna were thrilled, and others were waiting expectantly for their Messiah. Herod called a meeting of the leading priests and teachers of the religious law and inquired about the place where the Messiah was supposed to be born.

Wealthy, wise men have traveled from the East to come and worship this baby, a king from birth. That is incredible. He is already ruling and reigning before he has done one thing, evidenced by those who immediately recognize his kingship and worship him, and those who recognize it and are deeply disturbed by it.

The leading priests and teachers of religious law should have been as joyful as the shepherds seeking their Messiah. They knew exactly where He was supposed to be born. They can quote Micah 5:2 ESV. They knew He would be born in Bethlehem and would be '... one who is to be ruler in Israel.' So why aren't they ecstatic? Why are they deeply disturbed? They were supposed to be leading the people of Israel spiritually. Instead, hearing this threatened their power as it did Herod's. This is probably why they didn't get a visit from the angels proclaiming the birth.

Today's truth is this: to those who recognize their need for a Savior, Jesus is life. To those who seek their own power and authority and reject Him, He is a threat. We are the same as believers. "To those who are perishing, we are a dreadful smell of death and doom. But to those who are being saved, we are a life-giving perfume." (2 Corinthians 2:16 NLT)

Day 27

Herod was not happy to hear that there was a newborn King of the Jews. It seems that a baby would not threaten him, but if wealthy, wise men from the East are already seeking this king out, others would, too. Herod did not share power with anyone.

Herod met with the religious leaders and teachers and discovered where the child was born based on prophecy. Now, he must find out when the wise men saw the star. He has a private meeting with them and tells them to go to Bethlehem and find the child, then return and tell him so he can worship the child as well.

"After this interview, the wise men went their way. And the star they had seen in the east guided them to Bethlehem. It went ahead of them and stopped over the place where the child was. When they saw the star, they were filled with joy! They entered the house and saw the child with his mother, Mary, and they bowed down and worshiped Him. Then they opened their treasure chests and gave Him gifts of gold, frankincense, and myrrh." (Matthew 2:9-11 NLT)

The wise men worship next to the shepherds as Jesus lay in the manger in all the Christmas pageants, nativity scenes, and songs. But commentaries say that Jesus was probably anywhere from 6 to 18 months old when they arrived. They believe the star may have appeared on the night of Jesus' birth, and it would have taken the wise men several months to travel to see Him. Interestingly, the star they had originally seen in the

East now guided them to Bethlehem and the specific place where the child was. The Passion Translation commentary on verse 2:10 says, "The Greek is hard to translate since it contains so many redundant words for joy in this verse. It is literally, 'They rejoiced with a great joy exceedingly.' They were ecstatic." This was no mere star to them.

It is also believed that there were several wise men, not just three, as we usually depict them. It is probably because there were three gifts. Many have noted that the three gifts had special significance. The gold represented royalty, frankincense represented divinity, and myrrh represented His death. Still, most believe that while we can attribute these to Jesus now, the wise men were probably unaware of these things and only brought the lavish gifts to honor a king, which was the custom, especially in the East. More than lavish gifts, they gave Him their worship. The picture of wealthy, learned men with gifts around them, bowing to worship this small child as king, is an amazing picture to imagine.

When the wise men departed, they were warned in a dream not to return to Herod, so they went home another way. I wonder if they already suspected Herod had other motives for wanting their information. Whether or not they did, they were obedient to the warning and not complicit in Herod's plans.

Today's truth is a quote from Charles Spurgeon: "We see a wonderful pattern: Those who look for Jesus will see Him: those who truly see Him will worship Him: those who worship Him will consecrate their substance to Him."

Day 28

"After the wise men were gone, an angel of the Lord appeared to Joseph in a dream. 'Get up! Flee to Egypt with the child and his mother,' the angel said. 'Stay there until I tell you to return, because Herod is going to search for the child to kill him.' That night Joseph left for Egypt with the child and Mary, his mother, and they stayed there until Herod's death. This fulfilled what the Lord had spoken through the prophet: 'I called my Son out of Egypt.'" (Matthew 2:13-15 NLT)

Once again, we see Joseph given instructions on what to do, and once again, we see his quick obedience. It's easy to see Joseph as a background character because there isn't much written about him except for the first two chapters of Matthew and Luke. Mary needed only to believe, and she conceived by the Holy Spirit, but Joseph needed to believe and obey. He needed to do what God told him to do, rather than relying on his own wisdom and understanding.

If we take a hard look at the instructions to Joseph to take Mary and the child to Egypt, he could have had many questions. Egypt was known for its paganism, and it certainly didn't have a great track record for God's people. It wouldn't be easy to go to Egypt and settle his family there. But Joseph had trusted the Lord this far, and He had always come through, even to the point of providing the resources they needed to travel and settle in this foreign land without financial hardship. Of course, the threat of a jealous king who was intent on coming to kill the child would have been quite enough to spur someone to jump into action. Joseph left that very night. He didn't take a few days to get things in order.

The next few verses tell us that Herod was furious when he realized the wise men did not return to him, but had gone another way. In his rage, he sent soldiers to kill all the male children in Bethlehem who were two years old and under. He based this on when the wise men said the star had first appeared.

"Herod's brutal action fulfilled what God had spoken through the prophet Jeremiah: 'A cry was heard in Ramah—weeping and great mourning. Rachel weeps for her children, refusing to be comforted, for they are dead.'" (Matthew 2:17-18 NLT)

This is the part of the story that has always broken my heart. I can't imagine living in the small town of Bethlehem, and one day, soldiers burst through my door, take my child, and kill him. There would be no explanation, and even if there was, how could you ever comprehend the cruelty and evil of it all? Herod didn't just take the lives of those two and under in Bethlehem, but the villages surrounding it as well. Herod had two of his own sons killed, so why would he even blink at the slaughter of these innocents? His jealousy, hatred, and ruthlessness had no bounds.

Today's truth is this: the world Jesus was born into was and still is in desperate need of a Savior.

Day 29

The story we discussed yesterday is not typically part of the sweet Christmas pageants we enjoy watching. The jealousy and hatred of a cruel king, leaving devastation in his wake as he tries to remove the threat posed by the newborn King he fears, seems in sharp contrast to the angels singing joyfully in the field while shepherds watch with awe. The worship around the manger, the majesty, and the treasure of the wise men are all the things we look to and remember as we celebrate the birth of Jesus.

The truth of this heinous part of the story is why Jesus had to come, why we needed God with us, and why it's such a joyous celebration. Sin and death had their grip on all men. They came into the earth, taking men captive from the moment Adam made his choice to disobey God's command.

"When Adam sinned, sin entered the world. Adam's sin brought death, so death spread to everyone, for everyone sinned. Yes, Adam's one sin brings condemnation for everyone, but Christ's one act of righteousness brings a right relationship with God and new life for everyone." (Romans 5:12 and 18 NLT)

In our first couple of days, we read in Isaiah 9 that the people who walk in darkness would see a great light. Jesus was and is that light.

"For a child is born to us, a son is given to us. The government will rest on His shoulders. And He will be called: Wonderful Counselor, Mighty God, Everlasting Father, Prince of Peace." (Isaiah 9:6 NLT)

This is why we don't dwell on the brutal action of Herod because no matter what he may have tried to do in his evil schemes, he could never change the plans and purposes of God. Evil will never prevail. While Herod lived, Joseph and Mary, along with Jesus, would be protected as they waited in Egypt.

Today's truth is that darkness is in the world, but the light of Jesus shines brighter and stronger.

Day 30

"When Herod died, an angel of the Lord appeared in a dream to Joseph in Egypt. 'Get up!' the angel said. 'Take the child and his mother back to the land of Israel because those who were trying to kill the child are dead.' So, Joseph got up and returned to the land of Israel with Jesus and His mother. But when he learned that the new ruler of Judea was Herod's son Archelaus, he was afraid to go there. Then, after being warned in a dream, he left for the region of Galilee. So, the family went and lived in a town called Nazareth. This fulfilled what the prophets had said: 'He will be called a Nazarene.'" (Matthew 2:19-23 NLT)

Herod dies, and the angel tells Joseph to return to Israel. It's possible that Joseph thought of moving to Jerusalem, which you'd think would be a good place for the Messiah to grow up and be educated. The temple, the religious leaders, and the priests were there. Once Joseph entered Israel, he heard of the new ruler and likely learned of his cruelty and wickedness, similar to that of his father.

If you recall, Nazareth is the same village where God sent the angel Gabriel to Mary in Luke 1:26. I can imagine Joseph and Mary being excited to return to Israel, their homeland. They could have planned to go to Jerusalem, get Jesus in with one of the top Rabbis, and build their life there, waiting for Jesus to rule and reign one day. But once they get closer, they hear about Herod's son. Suddenly, their plans could be taking Jesus right back into danger. God is not going to let them go too long without direction. I'm sure they were praying and asking for His help all along. Joseph has a dream warning him that his fears are well-founded. Did God instruct Joseph in his dream to go to Nazareth, or did He command him not to go to Jerusalem? So, Joseph and Mary decided to return to their hometown, where family and friends would surely help them build a good life until Jesus' time came. Whether God specifically told them to go or directed their hearts, their settling in Nazareth was God's plan all along.

The village of Nazareth wasn't just another little village. Charles Spurgeon says, "There is always some city or village or another whose inhabitants seem to be the butt of every joke and the object of scorn. The people of such places are thought to be low, uncultured, and not very smart. That is the kind of place Nazareth was."

Why would God the Father have Jesus grow up in this despised town? Was it just the beginning of the fulfillment of these words in Isaiah 53:3 NLT? "He was despised and rejected—a man of sorrows, acquainted with deepest grief." Maybe it was a perfect place to hide Jesus until His time came.

"When Jesus' parents had fulfilled all the requirements of the law of the Lord, they returned home to Nazareth in Galilee. There, the child grew up healthy and strong. He was filled with wisdom, and God's favor was on Him." (Luke 2:39-40 NLT)

Today's truth is that it doesn't matter who you are or where you come from; if you follow God, He can fulfill His purposes and plans through you.

The Story Continues

Thank you for joining me as we unwrapped the Christmas Story. We are far from the end of all that could be discovered and learned from this amazing, ancient account. Like me, I hope you've seen something new and have grown in a deeper understanding of the message of Christ's birth.

The overall truth is that the Word of God is living and offers new and amazing insights every time we take the time to read it and dig deeper for what He wants to show us.

If you've enjoyed discovering new insights in God's Word with me, I'd love to invite you to read the book I co-wrote with my friend Michelle Jackson, *Ravenous, Hungry for God's Word*. The **Ravenous Method** we share there is the same approach I used to explore these powerful scriptures about Jesus.

Merry Christmas!

Debbie

References

David Guzik, https://enduringword.com/bible-commentary/isaiah-9/

John Calvin, *Commentary on a Harmony of the Evangelists, Matthew, Mark, and Luke*, Vol. 1, trans. William Pringle (Edinburgh: Calvin Translation Society, 1845), 108.

Charles Spurgeon, A summarization of Spurgeon's teachings, connecting it to his commentary on the wise men seeking Jesus in Matthew 2. https://enduringword.com/bible-commentary/matthew-2/

Charles Spurgeon, "The Nazarene and the Sect of the Nazarenes," Sermon No. 1632, preached at the Metropolitan Tabernacle on June 9, 1881.

About the Author

Debbie Kirkland makes her home in Austin, Texas, with her husband, Van. Married for over 40 years, they've raised three wonderful children and now share life with their black standard poodle, Captain. Debbie is also the co-author, with Michelle Jackson, of *Ravenous, Hungry for God's Word*. The approach to reading and delving deeper into Scripture from that book is what stirred her heart to write this 30-day devotional, inviting others to discover fresh meaning and hope in the Christmas story.

www.ingramcontent.com/pod-product-compliance
Lightning Source LLC
Chambersburg PA
CBHW060426050426
42449CB00009B/2149